Pebble® Plus

How to Build
Tornado
in a Bottle

Hands-On SCIENCE FUN

by Lori Shores

Consulting Editor: Gail Saunders-Smith, PhD

Consultant: Ronald Browne, PhD
Department of Elementary & Early Childhood Education
Minnesota State University, Mankato

CAPSTONE PRESS
a capstone imprint

Pebble Plus is published by Capstone Press,
1710 Roe Crest Drive, North Mankato, Minnesota 56003.
www.capstonepub.com

 Books published by Capstone Press are manufactured with paper
containing at least 10 percent post-consumer waste.

Library of Congress Cataloging-in-Publication Data
Shores, Lori.
 How to build a tornado in a bottle / by Lori Shores.
   p. cm.—(Pebble Plus. Hands-on science fun)
 Summary: "Simple text and full-color photos instruct readers how to build a tornado in a bottle and explain the science
behind the activity"—Provided by publisher.
 Includes bibliographical references and index.
 978-1-4296-4493-8 (library binding)
 978-1-4296-5577-4 (paperback)
 1. Tornadoes—Experiments—Juvenile literature. I. Title. II. Series.
 QC955.2.S54 2011
 551.55'3078—dc22   2010013585

Editorial Credits
Jenny Marks, editor; Juliette Peters, designer; Laura Manthe, production specialist; Sarah Schuette;
   photo shoot direction; Marcy Morin, scheduler

Photo Credits
All photos by Capstone Studio: Karon Dubke except: Dreamstime: Chris White, 17; Shutterstock: Jhaz Photography,
   cover, back cover (background), 1, 2–3, 22, 23, 24, Rafai Fabrykiewicz, 4–5

Note to Parents and Teachers

The Hands-On Science Fun set supports national science standards related to physical science.
This book describes and illustrates building a tornado in a bottle. The images support early
readers in understanding the text. The repetition of words and phrases helps early readers learn
new words. This book also introduces early readers to subject-specific vocabulary words, which
are defined in the Glossary section. Early readers may need assistance to read some words and to
use the Table of Contents, Glossary, Read More, Internet Sites, and Index sections of the book.

Printed in the United States of America in North Mankato, Minnesota.
062014   008214R

Table of Contents

Safety Note:
Please ask an adult for help in building your tornado in a bottle.

Getting Started

The rain pours

and the wind roars.

Tornadoes can be scary.

But there's nothing scary

about a tornado in a bottle.

2 clear 2-liter plastic
bottles, clean

duct tape

3 cups (¾ liter) of water

blue food coloring

Making a Tornado in a Bottle

First, remove the labels from two 2-liter bottles. Then mix a few drops of food coloring into 3 cups (¾ liter) of water. Pour the colored water into one of the bottles.

Place the empty bottle
upside-down on top
of the first bottle.
Line up the openings.

Use duct tape to cover

the necks of the bottles.

Wrap the tape tightly

so the bottles

won't come apart.

Turn the bottles over

so the water is on top.

Watch as the water moves

slowly to the bottom.

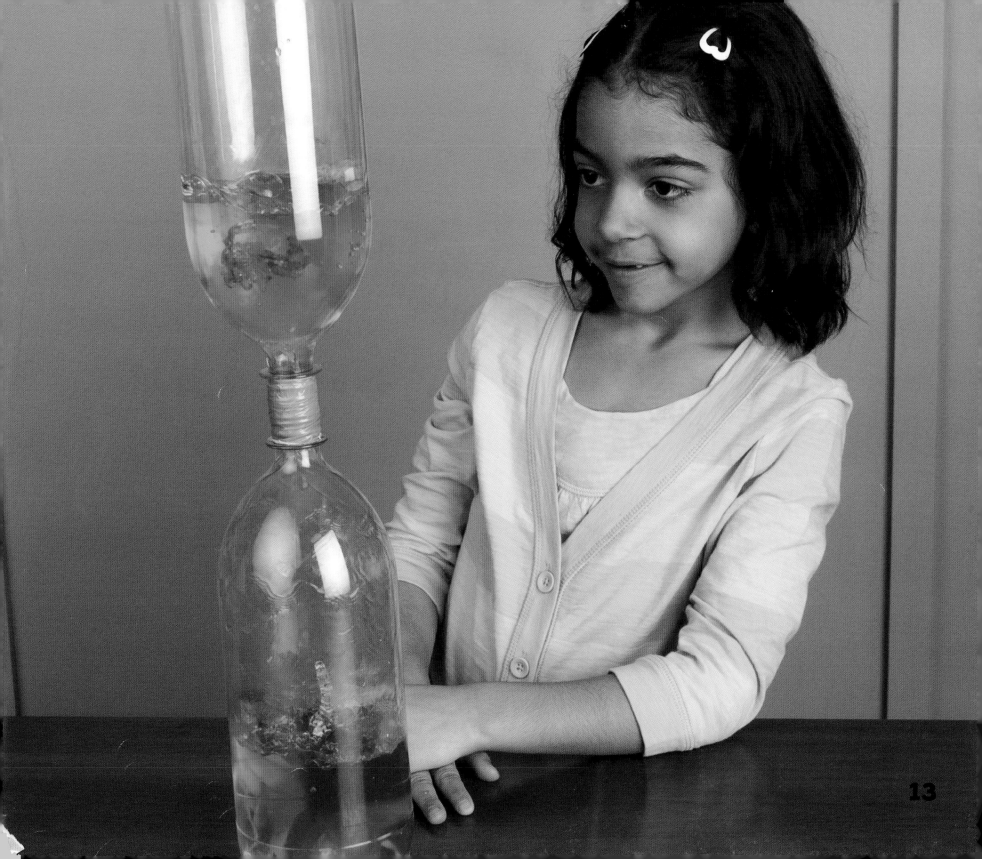

Turn the bottles over again.

Quickly swirl the bottles
in a circle a few times.
Watch as a tornado appears!

How Does It Work?

Real tornadoes happen

when hot air pushes up.

Wind whips around

a center point,

pulling cold air down.

wind

cold air

hot air

The tornado in the bottle works in a similar way. When the bottles are turned over, the air pushs up.

air

Swirling the bottles around
makes the water spin
around the center hole.
Like wind, the movement pulls
the water down.

Glossary

roar—to make a loud, deep noise

similar—alike

swirl—to quickly move around in circles

whip—to quickly move with great force

Read More

Gibbons, Gail. *Tornadoes!* New York: Holiday House, 2009.

VanCleave, Janice. *Janice VanCleave's Big Book of Play and Find Out Science Projects.* New York: Jossey-Bass, 2007.

Internet Sites

FactHound offers a safe, fun way to find Internet sites related to this book. All of the sites on FactHound have been researched by our staff.

Here's all you do:

Visit *www.facthound.com*

Type in this code: 9781429644938

Index

Word Count: 185
Grade: 1
Early-Intervention Level: 20